The MUTINY on the BOUNTY

PATRICK O'BRIEN

Walker & Company ❋ New York

"Land ho!" shouted the lookout.

Captain Bligh came on deck and gazed ahead. There it was at last—Tahiti. The sailors had heard fantastic stories about this island paradise on the far side of the world, and they were eager to see if the tales were true. Bligh had been there before, and he knew what to expect. But there was trouble brewing below deck, and what happened on the *Bounty* was something Bligh never expected.

William Bligh was the captain of the *Bounty*, a British naval ship. He was a difficult man to get along with. He raged at his sailors over small things, and he humiliated his officers by shouting insults at them in front of the crew.

But Bligh was one of the best seamen in the British Navy, and he was strong and brave in the face of danger. He ran a tight ship with strict discipline, but his punishments were usually fair.

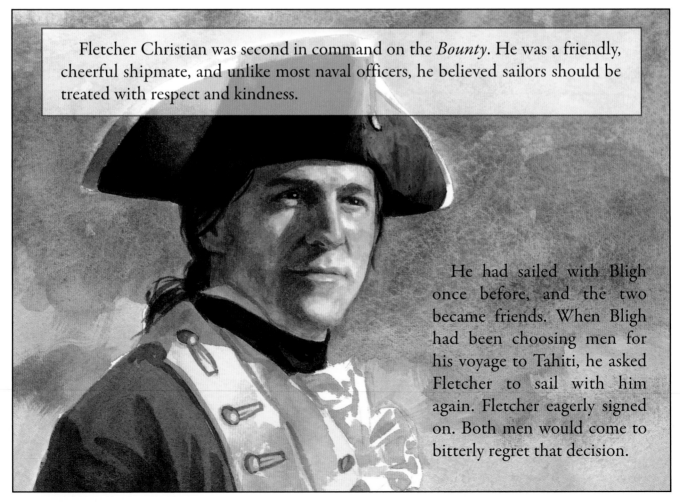

Fletcher Christian was second in command on the *Bounty*. He was a friendly, cheerful shipmate, and unlike most naval officers, he believed sailors should be treated with respect and kindness.

He had sailed with Bligh once before, and the two became friends. When Bligh had been choosing men for his voyage to Tahiti, he asked Fletcher to sail with him again. Fletcher eagerly signed on. Both men would come to bitterly regret that decision.

In December of 1787, the *Bounty* had left England on a very unusual mission. Captain Bligh was to sail the ship to Tahiti, collect hundreds of newly sprouted breadfruit trees, and then deliver the little trees to the Caribbean Islands, where they could provide food that was cheap, nutritious, and easy to grow.

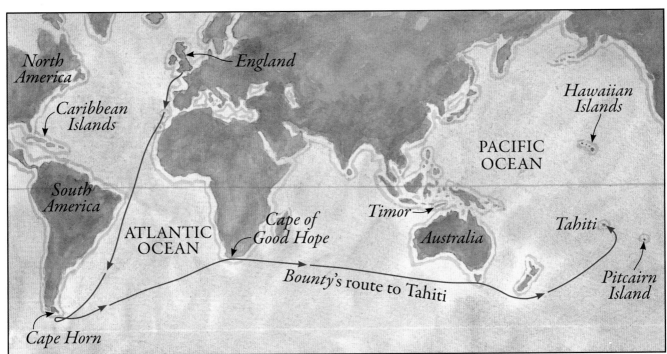

North America

England

Caribbean Islands

Hawaiian Islands

PACIFIC OCEAN

South America

Timor

ATLANTIC OCEAN

Cape of Good Hope

Australia

Tahiti

Bounty's route to Tahiti

Pitcairn Island

Cape Horn

Breadfruit was the main food source for the islanders of Tahiti. It grew wild on trees, so the people never needed to farm. When the fruit is cooked, it has the texture and smell of fresh-baked bread.

The *Bounty* was a small ship—only about ninety feet long. There were forty-six men on board.

The sailors lived in the forecastle, which was the area below deck in the front part, or bow, of the ship. They slept in hammocks hanging from the ceiling. It was dark, smelly, and very crowded.

The officers lived in the rear part, or stern, of the ship. They each had a small cabin, only slightly bigger than their bed.

There were three boats on board the ship. The biggest one was called the launch.

The *Bounty* was armed with four small cannons.

Normally, the large cabin in the stern would be the captain's cabin. But on the *Bounty* it was filled with hundreds of pots for breadfruit trees. Captain Bligh had to sleep and eat in two other small cabins.

Captain Bligh, Fletcher Christian, and the other officers were in charge of the ship. They gave the orders, and the sailors did all the hard work of furling the sails, pulling the ropes, and countless other tasks.

A sailor's life was one of constant work, extreme discomfort, and severe discipline.

The food on board the *Bounty* was the same as on other British ships—pretty bad.

Hardtack was a hard bread that was made before the voyage and stowed in the ship. There were usually maggots crawling through the bread. When food ran low, the sailors ate the maggots, too.

Salt meat was beef or pork that was made to last for months by treating it with lots of salt. It was hard as a rock and had to be soaked in water before it could be eaten.

The sailors often got cheese, but it was usually smelly and moldy.

The officers' food was a bit better. They got fresh meat and vegetables more often than the sailors.

Captain Bligh had hoped to reach the Pacific Ocean by sailing west around Cape Horn at the bottom of South America. For a whole month, the *Bounty* tried to round the Cape but was blown back by monstrous waves caused from fierce storms of snow and sleet. Bligh finally turned around and headed east to reach the Pacific by sailing around Africa's Cape of Good Hope.

The captain was king on a British Navy ship. His word was law. The slightest questioning or disobedience by his men was swiftly and harshly punished.

In the British Navy at that time, men were punished by flogging. This meant they were lashed with a whip called a cat-o'-nine-tails. Sailors were given dozens of lashes for even small offenses, and their backs were left bloodied and scarred. But Captain Bligh disliked flogging, and he used it less often than most captains.

During the voyage to Tahiti, Bligh did have one of his sailors flogged. The man got twenty-four lashes for what Bligh said was "insolence and mutinous behavior," which means he disobeyed an order.

After ten months at sea, the *Bounty* at last reached the island of Tahiti. As the ship neared the beach, hundreds of delighted islanders jumped into canoes and paddled out to meet it, carrying gifts of bananas and coconuts. They scrambled up the *Bounty*'s sides, and the deck was soon crowded with people laughing and shouting and trading gifts.

The first time a ship had visited Tahiti was just twelve years earlier. Before that, the islanders had known nothing at all about what lay beyond the Pacific Ocean. The men who arrived in their big ships from across the sea were like visitors from another world.

When Captain Bligh, Fletcher Christian, and some of the others went ashore, the Tahitians treated them to parties and dancing, eating and drinking. The sailors had never seen such beautiful, friendly people. The islanders seemed to live for nothing but fun.

Tahiti was a land of plenty. No one was rich and no one was poor, and no one went cold or hungry. They spent their days swimming in the clear streams, playing, laughing, and singing.

The sailors were amazed to see the Tahitians riding waves on flat pieces of wood. The Pacific Islanders had invented surfing.

Most of the *Bounty*'s crew had lived their whole lives on cramped and smelly ships and in England's cold rains and fogs. They now found themselves on what Captain Bligh called "the finest island in the world," where graceful waterfalls fell from tall, green mountains into lush valleys, and the sound of clear running streams mixed with the scent of exotic flowers. To the *Bounty*'s men, Tahiti was a paradise on earth.

Some of the *Bounty*'s men stayed on the ship, while others lived on shore and began the business of collecting breadfruit trees and planting them in pots.

Many of the *Bounty*'s men fell in love with the beautiful island women.

Tahitian men had a custom of choosing a *taio*, or a good friend, who would be almost like a member of their family. They were quick to choose *taios* from among the *Bounty*'s men.

Fletcher Christian was so enchanted by Tahiti that he lived among the islanders and began to dress like them.

Bligh usually stayed on the ship, where the local chief and his wife visited him almost every day.

But the many charms of Tahiti were causing the men to get lazy and careless. Bligh stamped and raged at the breakdown of his careful discipline and order. He had several of the sailors flogged for disobedience, and he bitterly scolded Christian and the other officers.

Christian began to resent this insulting treatment from his friend.

After five months in Tahiti, the men prepared the *Bounty* for sailing.

The decks were crowded with gifts from the people of Tahiti: there were live hogs, goats, chickens, and plenty of bananas for everyone.

Each man had his own stash of dozens of coconuts.

And in the large cabin, carefully stowed in special racks, there were more than a thousand potted breadfruit trees.

Hoisting the anchor and setting the sails, the men of the *Bounty* made their good-byes and sailed from paradise. Many of them would never make it home. The trouble was about to begin.

After leaving Tahiti, Bligh's angry outbursts got worse. He lost his self-control and exploded in fury over minor things.

Fletcher Christian got the worst of it. He wasn't allowed to talk back to his captain, but he quietly seethed with anger and humiliation.

During one rant Bligh called Christian a "cowardly rascal." In those days, insults to a gentleman's honor were very serious. Back in England, a man who was called a coward would probably have challenged his accuser to a duel. But on a Navy ship, the captain could say whatever he liked.

Although a captain was not allowed to flog an officer, an insult to an officer's honor could hurt as much as a lashing from the "cat."

One morning Captain Bligh came on deck and noticed that his pile of coconuts seemed a little smaller than it had been the night before. He flew into a rage, brought everyone on deck, and demanded to know if they had stolen any of his coconuts.

Christian replied, "I hope you don't think me so mean as to have stolen yours."

Bligh shot back, "Yes, you hound, I do. You scoundrels, you are all thieves." He threatened to make life so hard for the men that half of them would jump overboard.

Fletcher Christian finally snapped. He couldn't take any more abuse from his former friend. At first, he began to build a raft and planned to float off to an island. But then he changed his mind. He decided to take the ship. This would be mutiny, the worst crime in the Navy. There was just one punishment for mutiny—death by hanging.

It was before dawn. All was quiet. Christian whispered his plans to a few sailors who he knew would be willing to join him. Then the murmur went through the *Bounty*—"Christian is seizing the ship! Are you with us?" Breaking into the arms locker, the men got some guns. Then they crept down to the cabin where the captain lay asleep.

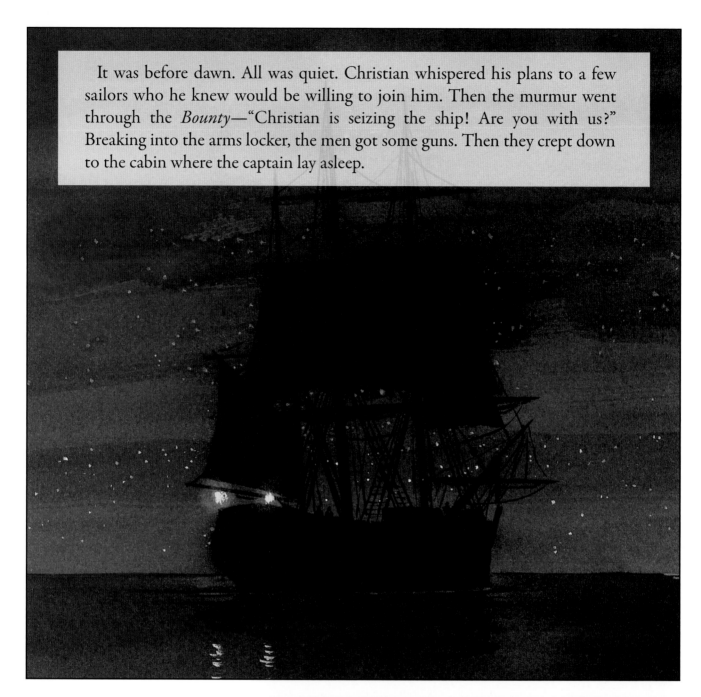

Bligh awoke to find five angry faces staring down at him.

"What is the meaning of this violence?" he demanded.

"Hold your tongue, sir," said Christian.

The men forced Bligh up the ladder to the deck.

"Murder!" Bligh shouted. "Murder!"

Now everyone on board was awake and there was much confused shouting and cursing. Some of the men were brandishing weapons and jeering at the captain, but other men were holding back, unsure of whose side they were on.

Bligh was shouting to anyone who would listen, "Knock Christian down!"

Christian, with a wild look in his eyes, pointed a bayonet at Bligh's chest and shouted, "*Mamoo!*" (which means "shut up" in the Tahitian language).

Many of the mutineers wanted to kill the captain, but Christian shouted them down. He ordered that Bligh be sent away in one of the ship's boats, along with any men who were still loyal to him.

The launch was lowered, and Christian was dismayed to see how many men chose to go with the captain. The boat became so crowded that some loyal sailors were forced to stay on the ship.

Bligh was allowed to get dressed. As he stood with Christian on the deck, he could see that the launch was far too overloaded and that the men would probably die from drowning or starvation.

"Think about what you are doing, Mr. Christian," said Bligh. "I have a wife and four children in England and you have danced my children on your knee."

"It is too late," replied Christian. "You have treated me like a dog all the voyage and I have been in hell."

Amid the shouts and taunts of the mutineers, Bligh climbed down into the crowded boat.

As the sun rose over a peaceful sea, Captain Bligh watched his ship sail slowly over the horizon. He was adrift on the vast Pacific Ocean with eighteen forlorn men, and only a small boat between them and the bottom of the ocean.

Bligh could see steam rising from the volcanic crater of an island over the horizon. He needed to find food and water, so he steered for the steam.

The men went ashore, but the people of the island were not friendly like the Tahitians. Dozens of natives began crowding around the men, jostling them and threatening to kill them. Bligh ordered his men back into the boat, then he drew his sword and slowly pushed through the hostile crowd. He reached the boat just as the natives began to attack.

The boat's anchor was still stuck on the beach. One of the men tried to free it, but the natives struck him down and killed him. Bligh slashed the anchor rope, and the men began rowing desperately as the natives chased them in canoes and hurled stones at them.

After their narrow escape, Bligh decided that it was too dangerous to stop at another island inhabited by natives. They would have to sail all the way to the island of Timor, the closest European settlement. But that was about 3,600 miles away, and there were no maps on board.

Bligh knew that it would take weeks to reach Timor, if they could make it at all. But there was very little food on the boat. Bligh gave each man a tiny amount of food each day and hoped it would last.

One day, they managed to snatch a bird out of the air. They divided it eighteen ways and ate it.

They were so hungry, they ate the bones, the beak, and the feet. They even ate the fish digesting in the bird's stomach.

Most of the time, they sailed through fierce storms. Huge waves threatened to break over the boat and sink it instantly. Seawater splashed in over the low sides, so the men could never stop desperately bailing water out. They were constantly wet, and the nights were bitter cold.

After a few weeks the men were so starving, exhausted, and cold that Bligh thought many of them would die.

After an agonizing month at sea, Bligh landed on a small, deserted island. The men were so weak many of them could not stand up. But they managed to find a little food and began to feel a bit better.

On this island, Bligh almost suffered another mutiny! The ship's carpenter, Matthew Purcell, had been making trouble throughout the voyage. Bligh scolded him and called him a scoundrel, to which Purcell replied, "I am not a scoundrel, sir, I am as good a man as you are!"

Talking back to a captain or refusing an order was close to mutiny, and Bligh was not about to let it happen again. He grabbed a sword and challenged Purcell to fight. Purcell backed down.

After six days on the island, the men climbed back in the boat. There were still more than a thousand miles to go.

Forty-eight days after the mutiny, Bligh finally sailed into the harbor at Timor. He wrote later, "Our bodies were nothing but skin and bones, our limbs were full of sores, and we were clothed in rags. As tears of joy and gratitude flowed down our cheeks, the people of Timor beheld us with a mixture of horror, surprise and pity."

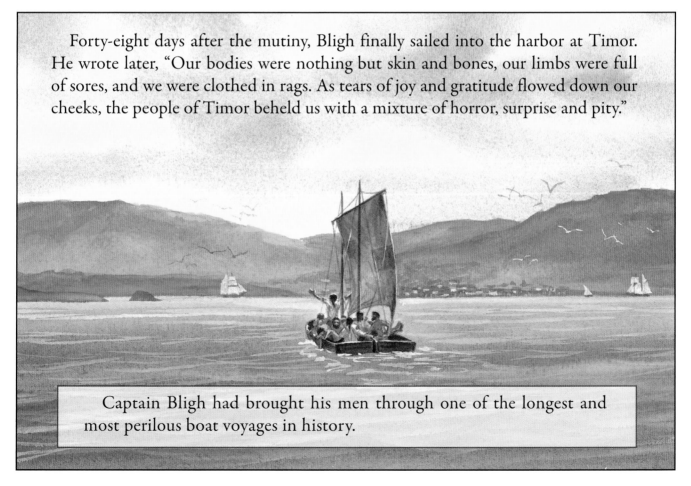

Captain Bligh had brought his men through one of the longest and most perilous boat voyages in history.

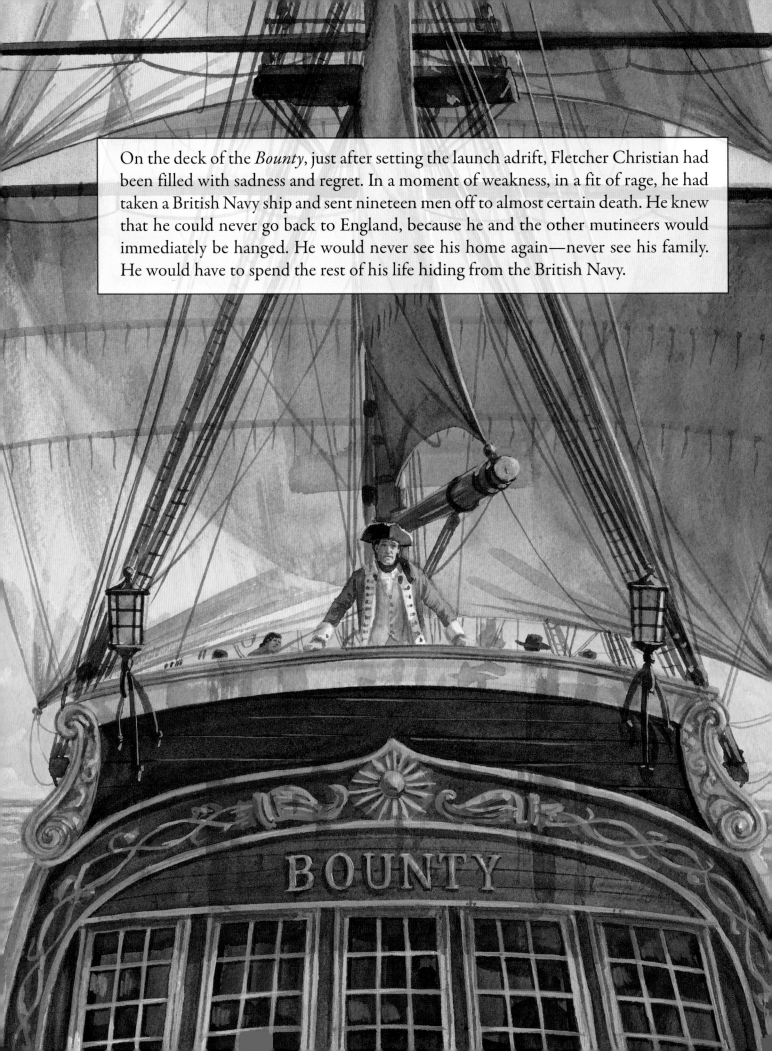

On the deck of the *Bounty*, just after setting the launch adrift, Fletcher Christian had been filled with sadness and regret. In a moment of weakness, in a fit of rage, he had taken a British Navy ship and sent nineteen men off to almost certain death. He knew that he could never go back to England, because he and the other mutineers would immediately be hanged. He would never see his home again—never see his family. He would have to spend the rest of his life hiding from the British Navy.

Christian sailed the *Bounty* back to Tahiti, but he knew he couldn't stay there. It was the first place the British Navy would look in its hunt for the mutineers.

But there were nine mutineers who decided to stay on the island and take their chances. There were also seven men who had not been part of the mutiny, but hadn't fit in the launch. These men also stayed on Tahiti. They were sure that someday a British ship would come for them.

Christian and eight of the mutineers set off in the *Bounty* along with twelve Tahitian women, six Tahitian men, and one baby. They were in search of a new home—a place where they could hide away from the rest of the world and the long arm of British law.

After sailing the Pacific for four months, they found the perfect island. It was, and still is, one of the most remote places in the world—Pitcairn Island.

The men unloaded everything from the ship that would be useful on the island, and carried it up a steep slope they named the Hill of Difficulty. At the top, they made tents using the *Bounty*'s sails.

A few days later, the men set the *Bounty* on fire.
Now they were stranded. They could never leave.

The mutineers started tiny farms and began families with the Tahitian women.

Fletcher Christian and his Tahitian wife, Mauatua, had a baby boy. They named him Thursday October Christian, because he was born on a Thursday in October.

Christian spent much of his time depressed and brooding in a shallow cave up in a cliff. His rash decision on that dark, still morning on the *Bounty* had caused him to be marooned on this tiny island for the rest of his life.

The mutineers were a rough bunch. They began feuding with each other and with the Tahitian men. Soon they started killing each other out of jealousy and revenge.

One day, while he was working in his field, Christian was shot. A Tahitian man had used one of the *Bounty*'s muskets to get revenge for killings by other mutineers. Four years after the mutiny that made him an outlaw, Fletcher Christian was dead.

Back in England, Captain Bligh had returned home—two and a half years after he had left.

Standing before the naval officials, he told his story of the mutiny on the *Bounty*. The officials were very angry about his loss of a ship, though they could not help but admire his amazing voyage in the launch.

The Navy was determined to catch the mutineers. Captain Edward Edwards was sent to the Pacific in the *Pandora* to round them up. Edwards sailed first to Tahiti, where he captured all the *Bounty* men who were still on the island.

Edwards locked all the men in chains on the *Pandora*, even the ones who had not been part of the mutiny.

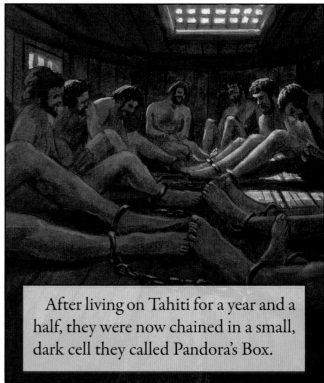

After living on Tahiti for a year and a half, they were now chained in a small, dark cell they called Pandora's Box.

Then Edwards sailed the Pacific for three months in search of Fletcher Christian and the rest of the mutineers. He never found them.

After all that the *Bounty*'s men had been through, there was still one more calamity in their story. Near Australia, the *Pandora* struck a reef. She quickly filled with water and sank. Four of the *Bounty*'s men could not escape their chains and drowned. The remaining ten men, as well as the *Pandora*'s men, had to sail in the ship's boats to safety in Timor. There they were put in other ships and returned to England.

The Navy put the men on trial for mutiny. Three of them were found guilty and hanged. Although most of the men who had sailed on the *Bounty* came to sad ends, these three were the only men punished for the mutiny.

Nineteen years after the mutiny, a Captain Folger on the American ship *Topaz* spotted Pitcairn Island. Going ashore, he met a smiling eighteen-year-old youth named Thursday October Christian.

Thursday lived in a happy little community of one English man, eight Polynesian women, and the twenty-six children of the *Bounty* mutineers. The man's name was John Adams, and he was the only mutineer still alive.

Captain Folger had solved the mystery of what had happened to Fletcher Christian and the *Bounty*.

Today, about fifty people live on Pitcairn Island. Most of them are descendants of the mutineers. The rotted remains of the *Bounty* sit on the bottom of Bounty Bay. Thursday October Christian's house is still standing. Above it in the cliffs, Christian's Cave can still be seen. On this remote, rocky island in the vast blue Pacific, there are still living reminders of Fletcher Christian, Captain Bligh, and the mutiny on the *Bounty*.

Resources

Alexander, Caroline. *The Bounty*. New York: Penguin Books, 2003.

Bligh, William. *The Mutiny on Board HMS Bounty*. New York: New American Library, 1962.

Bligh, William. *Return to Tahiti: Bligh's Second Breadfruit Voyage*. Honolulu, HI: University of Hawaii Press, 1988.

Christian, Glynn. *Fragile Paradise: The Discovery of Fletcher Christian, Bounty Mutineer*. Boston: Little, Brown, 1982.

Dening, Greg. *Mr. Bligh's Bad Language: Passion, Power, and Theatre on the Bounty*. New York: Cambridge University Press, 1992.

Hough, Richard Alexander. *Captain Bligh and Mister Christian*. Annapolis, MD: Naval Institute Press, 1972.

Howarth, David. *Tahiti: A Paradise Lost*. New York: The Viking Press, 1983.

Moorehead, Alan. *The Fatal Impact: The Invasion of the South Pacific, 1767-1840*. New York: Harper & Row, 1987.

Wahlroos, Sven. *Mutiny and Romance in the South Seas: A Companion to the Bounty Adventure*. Topsfield, MA: Salem House Publishers, 1989.

It's all for Alex

Copyright © 2007 by Patrick O'Brien

First published in the United States of America in 2007 by
Walker Publishing Company, Inc.
Distributed to the trade by Holtzbrinck Publishers

For information about permission to reproduce selections from
this book, write to Permissions, Walker & Company,
104 Fifth Avenue, New York, New York 10011

Library of Congress Cataloging-in-Publication Data
O'Brien, Patrick.
The mutiny on the Bounty / Patrick O'Brien.
p. cm.
Includes bibliographical references.
ISBN-10: 0-8027-9587-0 • ISBN-13: 978-0-8027-9587-8 (hardcover)
ISBN-10: 0-8027-9588-9 • ISBN-13: 978-0-8027-9588-5 (reinforced)
1. Bounty Mutiny, 1789—Juvenile literature. 2. Bounty (Ship) — Juvenile literature. 3. Bligh, William, 1754-1817—Juvenile literature. 4. Christian, Fletcher, 1764-1793—Juvenile literature. 5. Oceania—Description and travel—Juvenile literature. 6. Ocean travel—History—18th century—Juvenile literature. 7. Mutiny—Oceania—History—18th century—Juvenile literature. 8. Pitcairn Island—History—18th century—Juvenile literature. I. Title.
DU20.O27 2006   910.4'5—dc22   2006010193

The illustrations for this book were created using watercolor and gouache on watercolor paper.

Book design by Patrick O'Brien

Visit Walker & Company's Web site at www.walkeryoungreaders.com

Printed in China

2 4 6 8 10 9 7 5 3 1

All papers used by Walker & Company are natural, recyclable products
made from wood grown in well-managed forests. The manufacturing processes
conform to the environmental regulations of the country of origin.